Perfect Gift Wrapping Ideas

101 Ways to Personalize Your Gift
Using Simple, Everyday Materials

HIROE MIYAOKA

Ideas for making life fun!

From everyday casual gifts to presents for special occasions,
there's wrapping that expresses your feelings—like sentiments
of gratitude and congratulations—in style.

Full of ideas for splendid gift giving,
the wrapping lessons start here!

TUTTLE Publishing

Tokyo | Rutland, Vermont | Singapore

Contents

chapter
3

Wrapping with Handmade Materials

Special Tips

✳ The paper sizes required for all wrapping methods shown depend on the item being wrapped, its shape and your personal taste. For wrapping that requires non-standard size paper, the size needs are indicated, e.g. "one sheet big enough to go around the item vertically".

chapter
4

Techniques for Beautiful Gift Wrapping

Enjoying Wrapping in Everyday Life

Stylish wrapping is a given for special occasions, but it also warms the heart when used for everyday situations, such as giving a gift of home-made food or sharing something you've received. Use wrapping to say thank you: package up your feelings of appreciation along with a present.

Daily wrapping

Jam

Tart or Pie

How to wrap it

Jam
📦 p.49

Tart or Pie
🎁 p.90

Waffles

Chocolates

Package Homemade Treats Just Like in the Store

Well-made cookies and treats from your "home café" deserve to be shown off.
Jellies and tarts look fresh in see-through packaging, while chic wrapping
works for baked goods and chocolates.

How to wrap it

Waffles
📦 **p.50** 🎀 **p.88** 🎁 **p.86**

Chocolates
📦 **p.74** 🎀 **p.88**

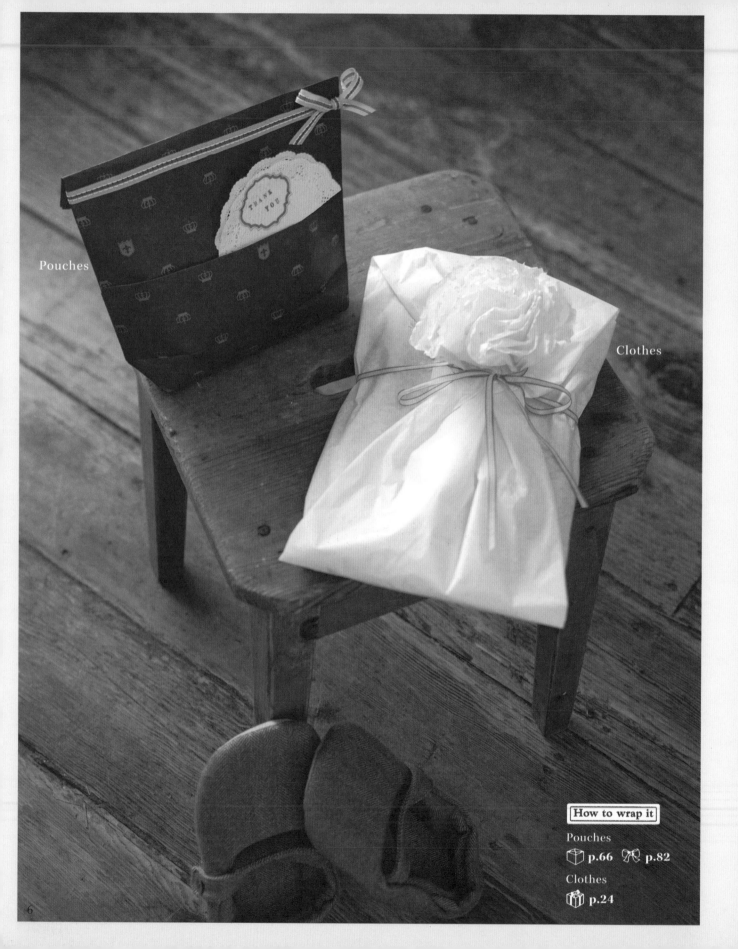

Pouches

Clothes

How to wrap it

Pouches
p.66 p.82

Clothes
p.24

6

Jewelry

How to wrap it
p.90

Handkerchiefs

How to wrap it
p.25 p.82

Stylish Wrappings for Handmade Gifts

Wrapping often conjures up images of a box all neatly packaged. But even without a box, there are many ways to package gifts so that the gift and the wrapping are in sync. For textiles, garments and other cloth items, match the soft feel of the fabric with light, airy wrapping paper. And for accessories, use the wrapping to bring out their beauty.

Share Fruit Around the Neighborhood in Style

If you've got produce to spare, make a present of it in these handmade bags with handles. Unassuming in appearance, they're sturdy enough to be used over and over, making them an appreciated bonus gift.

How to wrap it

p.66

Little Holiday Souvenirs for Friends

This sort of wrapping is quick and easy. Simply by changing the paper and ribbon you can achieve a variety of looks. Match the wrapping to suit the recipient's personality and taste!

How to wrap it

p.25

p.25   p.82   p.84

p.25   p.88   p.86

Wrap Flowers to Take to a Friend's Party

Whether they're grown in your own garden or bought from a shop, flowers can be dressed up beautifully when wrapped well. The trick is to choose paper and ribbon that complement the flowers. A wide ribbon adds a touch of luxury.

How to wrap it

p.45   p.82

Wrapping for a special day

How to wrap it

📦 p.78   🎀 p.31   🎁 p.84

A Birthday Gift for a Close Friend

A birthday is a special day that comes just once a year, so a birthday present should be exceptionally well wrapped. For a woman, add a corsage made from lace ribbon to a gift wrapped in girly pink packaging. Tickets presented in a decorated handmade envelope are a cute gift idea too!

How to wrap it

📦 p.62

11

How to wrap it
 p.91

Matching the Giftwrap to the Recipient

When giving a formal or ceremonial gift to parents or seniors, a gorgeously presented gift box is a good choice. On the other hand, a casual approach is fine for younger friends. For men, remember to play down color and decoration. The wrapping paper used for this necktie is simply a page of newspaper that has been painted. Even if it tears, it won't matter—well, not too much.

For kids

Book

CD

How to wrap it

Book 🎁 **p.92**

CD 📦 **p.25** 🎀 **p.88** 🎁 **p.86**

Ties

Wine

How to wrap it

p.92

Clothes, Bibs, Toys

When you want to give an array of cute items at once, try arranging them in a basket wrapped in cellophane and ribbon. Cellophane is an excellent material—it's simple to use yet lends a professional look.

Making Kids' Christmas Presents Fun

A Christmas tree takes over the wrapping! Decorate the tree however you like.

How to wrap it

🎁 **p.93**

Grown-up Valentine's Day Gifts

Wax paper creates a simple, chic air. Set yourself apart from your rivals with this sophisticated wrapping!

For those all-important chocolates…

How to wrap it

📦 **p.41**

How to wrap it

📦 **p.76** 🎀 **p.88**

Tips and Tricks for Beautiful Wrapping

When you're putting your heart into your gift giving, you want the wrapping to look as neat as possible. Mastering these little tricks will make a real difference.

Match paper to the size of the gift and cut with a blade

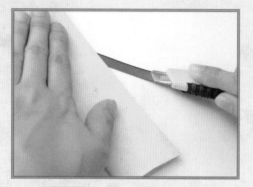

Once you've decided how to wrap something, measure the paper to match and cut it to the right size with a retractable utility knife. Extending the blade so that it's quite long will give a better cut.

Peel off double-sided tape slowly

Making use of double-sided tape to join paper is a wrapping fundamental. When using tape, peel off a bit of the backing before holding the paper in place over it, then slowly remove the rest of the backing.

For margin folds, neat lines are a must

A margin fold involves making a narrow fold along the edge of the paper inwards to form a neat line. Fold carefully to achieve a straight line.

Tie ribbons tautly and puff out to finish

When finishing wrapping with a ribbon, a firm knot and a full bow give a neat result. When tying in a bow, tug on the back of the right loop and the front of the left.

Basic Lessons in Gift Wrapping

Wrapping starts with the gift and the material in which it is to be presented. Here, we introduce the perfect materials and equipment needed for stylish wrapping, along with methods for wrapping various items for a clever result—no special techniques required.

Tools for Wrapping

The basic tools you will need are a retractable utility knife, double-sided tape, cellophane tape and four kinds of scissors. Other special tools will also be introduced.

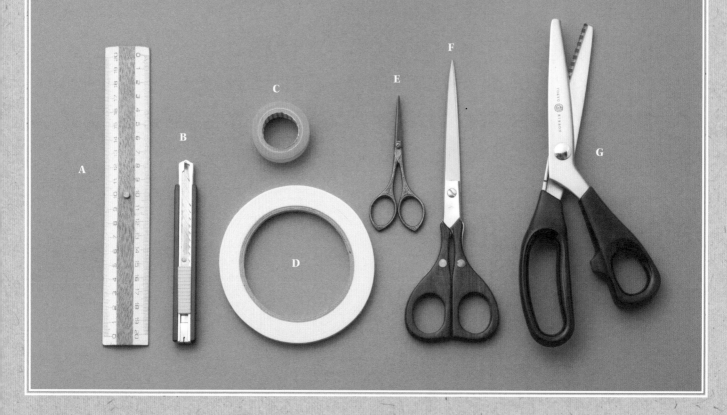

A Ruler
Handy for accurately measuring paper sizes, creating folds in paper and so on.

B Cutter
Used for cutting paper to the right size. When cutting paper, the blade is extended out, so choose a small knife with a supple blade.

C Cellophane Tape
Useful for joining parts that won't be seen or to secure pieces temporarily. It's not attractive, so it's better not to use it at the finishing stages.

D Double-sided Tape
Used for joining wrapping and attaching paper and the like. It is recommended to use a narrow type of about ¼–⅜ in (7–10mm) in width. Tear off pieces with your hands to make it easier to remove the backing.

E Craft Scissors
Used for cutting ribbon and other fabric. If used for cutting tape or paper, the blades will become blunt, so keep them to use for fabric only.

F Scissors
Used for cutting paper, clipping into bags, cutting paper ties and so on.

G Pinking Shears
With their special chevron edged blades, these shears are used for cutting notch patterns along the edges of ribbon and paper. If used on fabric, they prevent fraying.

Wrapping Materials

When choosing wrapping materials, keep in mind the gift, the recipient, and the occasion. Try wrapping in a variety of materials, from wrapping paper to materials close to hand.

A Plain and Patterned Paper
A wide variety of paper is sold for wrapping. There are plenty of seasonal patterned papers too, such as for Christmas.

B Crepe Paper
This paper is processed to have wrinkles. There is some stretch to it, so it's good to use when wrapping irregularly shaped objects.

C Non-woven Fabric
Made from synthetic fibers and similar to fabric, this can be used to softly wrap irregularly shaped objects.

D Glassine Paper
This thin, transparent paper is used for packaging medicines but is also recommended for wrapping food and other items.

E Wax Paper
This paper has a wax coating which gives it shine. It's water resistant, making it good for wrapping flowers.

F Craft Paper
Used as packing material, this paper can be used for casual wrapping.

G Tissue Paper
Often found layered between garments, tissue paper can be used for wrapping clothes and other soft items.

H Cellophane
For wrapping a parcel whose contents are on display. Patterned and colored types are also available, as are cellophane bags.

I Materials to Hand
Baking paper, paper napkins and other items on hand also work well as wrapping paper.

Tying and Binding Materials

Once wrapping is complete, finish it off with a ribbon or cord. The combination of materials used makes a big difference to the final look.

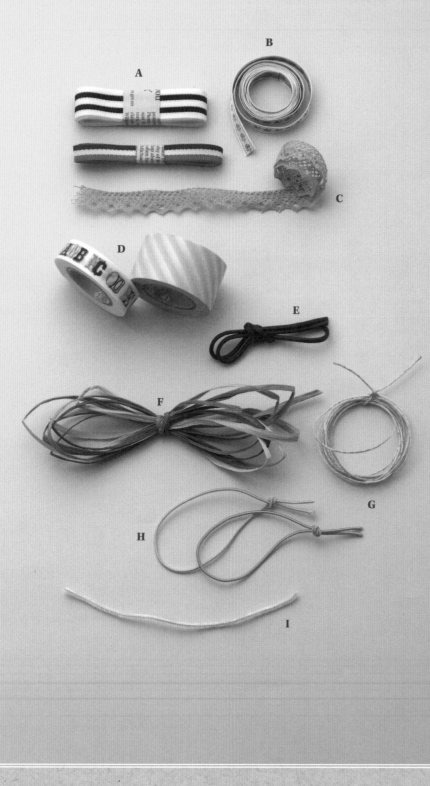

A Ribbons
There are many kinds of ribbon, including glossy types and types with wire inserts. Choose the ribbon depending on the feeling you want to create.

B Two-sided Ribbons
There is a different pattern on the outer and reverse sides of this kind of ribbon, so take special care when tying a bow (see p82).

C Lace Ribbons
Use lace ribbons made from materials such as cotton and linen to add a girly touch.

D Washi Tape
The variety of colors and patterns on the market make this the perfect accent for wrapping.

E Cords
Perfect for wrapping with a simple, natural effect. It is available in various materials including paper and a range of fibers.

F Raffia
Thin paper is drawn out to form paper raffia. Processed varieties made from natural raffia palm are also available.

G Linen cords
Originally used for securing parcels, linen cord makes the perfect finishing touch for a casual look.

H Elastic Cord
Colored elastic cord can be used in place of ribbon for a "pop" finish.

I Pipe Cleaners
Made from fine wire, a pipe cleaner can easily be twisted around the top of a bag to secure it.

Decorating Materials and Little Extras

Little elements like these can add originality and style to your gift.

A Seals and Stickers
Can be used to keep the opening of a bag closed or the ends of ribbon in place. Old stamps add a sense of romance.

B Dried Flowers
Adding just one flower to a parcel wrapped and tied with ribbon makes a gift seem extra special.

C Artificial Flowers
Create artificial flowers for wrapping, or original corsages (see p31)

D Lace Paper (Doilies)
Although intended for use with sweets and baked goods, doilies are great layered over wrapping just as they are to create an antique effect.

E Cards
Postcards and message cards are also a lovely accent to add to wrapping.

F Ornaments
Thread cord through buttons and charms to tie them to parcels, or glue them onto wrapping to create an accent.

G Tags
The addition of a tag creates a stylish parcel. They are available in a variety of materials—or make your own (see p54)

H Boxes
Available in paper, plastic and other materials and in a variety of shapes, boxes suit formal gifts.

I Bags
Handy for simple packaging, bags are available in a wide range of materials, sizes and types.

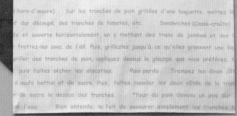

Make Your Gift Wrapping Personal

A gift is the embodiment of feelings of gratitude or congratulations, and the wrapping around it is the spice that enhances those emotions. So when wrapping a gift, start by considering the recipient and the reason for giving.

STEP 1

Consider the gift and the recipient

Wrapping differs significantly depending on whether the gift is for a wedding or other formal occasion, or is something casual such as a gift from your travels or food that is being shared. Also keep in mind your relationship with the recipient as well as their personality when deciding on wrapping.

STEP 2

Consider the wrapping materials

The gift item itself plays the main role here. For instance, a casual stole should be wrapped in soft tissue paper. More formal attire should be placed in a box and wrapped in flamboyant paper.

STEP 3

Consider decorations

In the world of wrapping, the ribbon rules. With so many varieties available, ribbons can create all kinds of looks and are popular with people of all ages. For casual gifts, consider cords, tape, tags and other materials.

STEP 4

Convey your feelings to someone special

Put your heart into your wrapping and show the recipient that you care. Don't focus too much on the technique —the most important thing is that your feelings go into the wrapping to make the recipient happy!

1 Lay the paper in a diamond shape.

2 Pinch in the paper at the base of the bottle to make pleats.

Wrinkles added to the paper lend a casual look

Craft Paper Bottle Wraps

Although craft paper was once used only as packaging material, depending on how it is used it can make for lovely wrapping. If scrunched up so that wrinkles form before it is used as wrapping, it can create a grown-up, antique air.

3 Lay the bottle on top of the paper and, starting at the edge, roll the paper around the bottle.

4 Work until about halfway around the base, gathering the pleats into one place.

MATERIALS: craft paper (width: 1.5–2 x circumference of bottle, length: 1–1.5 x bottle height of bottle), cord

Tissue Paper Garment Wraps

Tissue paper is very thin paper that is used as an inner layer when wrapping things like clothes. An item made from soft material and wrapped in airy layers makes an elegant, gentle impression. There are plenty of color variations!

MATERIALS: tissue paper x 2 sheets (width: 1.5–2 x the width of the item; length: length of the item plus enough to fold over), ribbon

1 Using two sheets of tissue paper together, lay the item for wrapping in the center and fold first the side to your left, then the side to your right over the item.

2 Fold in the end furthest from you, matching it up with the end closest to you.

3 Gather the ends together and tie with a ribbon. The photo shows a ribbon tied in a triple loop (see p88).

Wax Paper Stationery Wraps

Wax paper has a glossy charm all its own. As it doesn't take adhesives well, wax paper won't mix well with tape, but it's the perfect candidate for creating the classic string-tied parcel. It works well as a wrapping for any shaped item, so keep it in mind.

Variations

Play up wrinkles for a natural look

A bottle has been wrapped parcel-style and finished with an original decorative tie.

Try a twisted top

A simple tweak to the basic steps behind this wrapping reaps results. First, fold up the base, followed by left and right sides, sliding the left edge in under the right, and finish by tying at the top.

MATERIALS: wax paper (width: width of item + breadth of item x 2 + 60% of width of item; length: height of item + 2 in [5cm]); linen cord

1 Place item in the center of the wax paper and fold over left and right sides.

2 Fold over the top of the paper in line with the item.

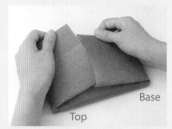

Base

Top

3 Slide the folded top section into the hollow of the base fold and tie with linen cord. The photo shows the cord tied in a crucifix style (see p84).

Glassine Paper Food Wrappers

This type of wrapping is recommended for bazaars and gatherings that call for handing out parcels of candy as party favors. Forming a carrot shape, the wrapping is finished off with a simple ribbon tie.

MATERIALS: glassine paper (cut into squares), ribbon
*Paper shown in the photo is 7 in (18cm) square

1 With the centerpoint of the bottom edge of the square glassine paper as a starting point, wind the paper to form a cone.

2 Tape in place and spoon in contents a little at a time.

3 Twist top and tie with a ribbon.

Put both sides of reversible paper into play

Crepe Paper & Kitchen Utensils

A wooden spatula and other kitchen utensils are wrapped simply in crepe paper. As it has some stretch to it, crepe paper is perfect for wrapping irregularly shaped objects. This parcel has been styled as a casual wedding gift with celebratory red as the accent.

Variations

Perfect for wrapping a mug!

This uses the same paper as the kitchen utensil parcel, but with the red side facing out. It's finished off using the twist and tie method (see p76).

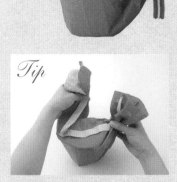

Tip

Shift the item from the center of the paper to the right by about the width of the item when you start wrapping. Gather paper on the right side and tie.

MATERIALS: crepe paper (for size, see "diagonal wrapping" on p72, allowing a bit more paper than usual for the pocket section)

∗The size and shape of the pocket will vary depending on factors such as the item being wrapped and the paper size. This wrapping is suited to flat, irregularly shaped items rather than boxes.

Tip

Follow the diagonal wrapping steps on p72 to wrap the item, then fold paper left on top outwards and over again to form pocket.

A lovely grown-up flamboyance that works for both men's and women's gifts

Washi Paper Umbrella Wraps

Traditional Japanese paper comes in a wide variety of designs and patterns. A fold-up umbrella gets a modern wrapping treatment thanks to a spin on the traditional Japanese style of a strip of paper and cord wound around the gift.

MATERIALS: washi paper (see "diagonal wrapping" on p72 for size details), plain washi paper (width: diameter of item + ⅞ –1¼ in (2–3cm); length: half of item's height), kumihimo cord

1 Wrap folding umbrella as per instructions for "diagonal wrapping" on p72.

2 Wind plain washi paper around the parcel and tape in place.

3 Tie kumihimo cord around parcel, over the top of the plain band of paper. The main photo shows the cord tied in a single loop (left) and triple loop (right) (see p88).

1 Place pot in center of fabric. Fold in fabric in front and behind pot by about ⅔ the height of the pot.

2 Tie sides, drawing up the fabric in front and behind as you go.

Approx. height of pot

3 Slip one end of fabric deep inside the other.

4 Check that the weight of the plant sits evenly, then tie handle with cord as shown in the photo.

Simple portability is the main point
Fabric Potted Plant Wrapper

As fabric is soft, it's perfect for wrapping irregularly shaped items. A traditional furoshiki cloth is the standard fabric used for wrapping, but the material shown in the photo is a dish towel. Make sure to place a saucer underneath the pot to catch any water before you wrap it.

MATERIALS: fabric (width: approx. pot diameter + height of pot x 5; length: approx. pot diameter + height of pot x 2), cord

29

Little Extras Touches for a Lovely Wrapping

These little touches that can be added to regular wrapping make a big difference when it comes to style. Exercise your personal taste when choosing items.

Narrow Ribbons

This arrangement is easily achieved by firmly winding narrow ribbon around and around a parcel. An interesting magazine picture of an elderly man is used as wrapping paper.

Variations

You don't have to stick to ribbon—cord can be used to wind around parcels too. The parcel on the left is decorated with a charm threaded onto linen cord, while leather cord has been used around the parcel on the right.

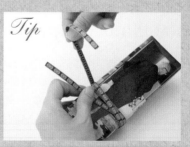

Tip

When working out where to place the ribbon, consider the parcel size and the pattern on the wrapping paper. Keep the ribbon taut at the edges of the item as you wrap it around.

Corsages

This original corsage is a super-fast project whose appeal lies in the fact that it can be created from a multitude of materials. The photo shows a corsage made from wax paper and newspaper.

Variations

Two colors of non-woven fabric are layered here to form flowers, but materials such as felt, fabric or lace ribbon could also be used.

1 Place two pieces of paper 12 in wide x 3 in (30cm x 8cm) long one on top of the other. For flowers with more volume, use as many layers of paper as you like.

2 Fold in half lengthways. Fold over twice from one end, repeating three times.

3 Cut the top of the paper into a semi-circle shape. This will form the flower's petals, so cut the shape as you like.

4 Open out the paper, slip a length of wire (or cord) down the center vertically and bend in half.

5 Holding the wire so it doesn't shift, gather the paper into a ring a little at a time.

6 Once the paper is bunched tightly, twist the wire or tie the cord to secure in place. Fold out the petals from the outside, working in.

Using Washi Tape

Washi tape is available in a variety of colors and designs.
It has the special characteristics of being able to be torn off
the roll by hand and removed easily and is simple to use.
Combine several different colors for a cute, pop finish.

Variations

Stamp words onto washi
tape (or even plain masking
tape) and stick it to parcels, or
use it to close bags. Use ink
formulated for use on glass
when stamping onto tape.

Stick lines of washi
tape on patterned
wrapping to create
original paper.

Tip

This photo frame has been
wrapped in transparent baking
paper with washi tape layered
over it. Tape easily comes off
baking paper, so the trick to this
look is to apply layers of tape a
little at a time.

Sealing Wax

Used in the West since olden times, sealing wax is perfect for giving a chic finish to wrapping. Choose a sealing stamp and find some wax to get started.

Eyelets

Eyelets are used to reinforce the area around holes. They are useful for a multitude of wrapping purposes including attaching tags and threading cord. An eyelet punch with interchangeable parts is recommended.

1 For wax with no wick, start by breaking off only the amount you will need.

2 Place wax on a spoon wrapped in aluminum foil and hold over candle flame.

1 Create hole using hole punch.

2 Insert eyelet into hole.

3 Once wax has melted, pour it over the area you wish to stamp.

4 Stamp into wax, pressing into flat part for a neat result.

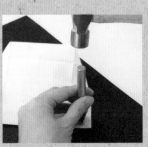

3 Place eyelet punch over eyelet on reverse side and tap from above.

＊Sealing stamps, wax and eyelet punches are available at larger stationery stores and craft supply stores. Eyelet punches are also available in a plier type.

Clear Plastic Bags—an All-purpose Wrapper

When it comes to cute wrapping of small items, clear plastic bags really pull their weight. They come in a wide range of sizes, and can even be found in dollar stores. Use them to show off a cute gift selection to full effect!

Add paper doily for a romantic look

Line the base of the bag with the paper doily. Run a cord around the mouth of the bag, folding plastic 2–3 times over cord, then lift ends of cord and tie together.

Create a tear-off paper opening

Cut paper to the width of the bag, fold in half and glue over mouth of bag. Run a rotary cutter used for sewing over the upper edge of paper to make perforations.

A pop-art touch for an array of bath goods

Cover a wire tie with your choice of paper to create an original tie. Place bath goods in bag so they are well balanced visually and secure the tie around the bag opening.

A grown-up air for a candle

Place tissue paper on the base of the bag, then place the candle on top and tie the bag closed. Fold the corners of the bag underneath and tape in place to create base.

Play with color to set off a candy selection

Glue candy to paper cut to the size of the bag, then slide paper into bag. Cut into the sides of a straw and sandwich mouth of bag in between, using tape to secure in place.

Make a tetra block for a small toy

Place toy and cotton balls for packaging in bag and form bag into a tetra block (see p41). Run ribbon along folded mouth of bag and tie ends.

chapter
2

Wrapping with Materials
You Have on Hand

In this section you will find ideas on how to use
items that are around the home or are easy to find
to create simple, cute wrapping. These are sure to
come in handy when wrapping casual gifts for
close friends or for packaging little presents.

Paper Bags Can Take on Many Shapes

Just a few touches and tweaks have transformed these little paper bags into all kinds of things. All the bags used were purchased at dollar stores. Stock up so that you have some handy when you need to give a little something.

A

B

C

A Prepare a flat bottomed paper bag and curling ribbon. Fold over flap of bag so lace pattern shows and tape to side of bag. Slide ribbon through gap between flap and bag and tie, then use blade of scissors to curl ends of ribbon (see p42).

B Prepare a flat bottomed paper bag and ribbon. Fold mouth of bag over twice, folding away from you. Clip into the left and right of the bag directly under the fold, cutting to about the width of the bag base (see photo, left). Fold clipped sections toward you to create collar (see photo, right).

C Prepare a flat bottomed paper bag and cord. Fold mouth of bag over twice, folding away from you, then create pleats by folding back and forth. Tie cord in V shape over center of bag (see p86). Pull the pleats into place to form a fan shape.

D Prepare a flat bottomed paper bag, cord and eyelets. Fold mouth of bag over once away from you. Insert eyelet into top right of bag (see p33). Run cord through eyelet. A photo shrunk on a photocopier has been stuck on as an accent.

Make a Newspaper Gift Box

When using newspaper as wrapping, the trick to giving it a chic finish is to use newspaper. For sharing out spices or foodstuffs, linen cord or embroidery thread tied around the gift adds a finishing touch.

Newspapers make excellent inexpensive wrapping!

MATERIALS: newspaper (cut into squares. Cut the lid section ¼–⅜ in [0.5–1cm] bigger than the corresponding base)

*The photos show three sizes of paper squares being used. Large: 7½ in/19cm (lid 7¾ in [19.5cm]) Medium: 6¾ in (17.5cm) Small: 5¾ in (14.5cm)

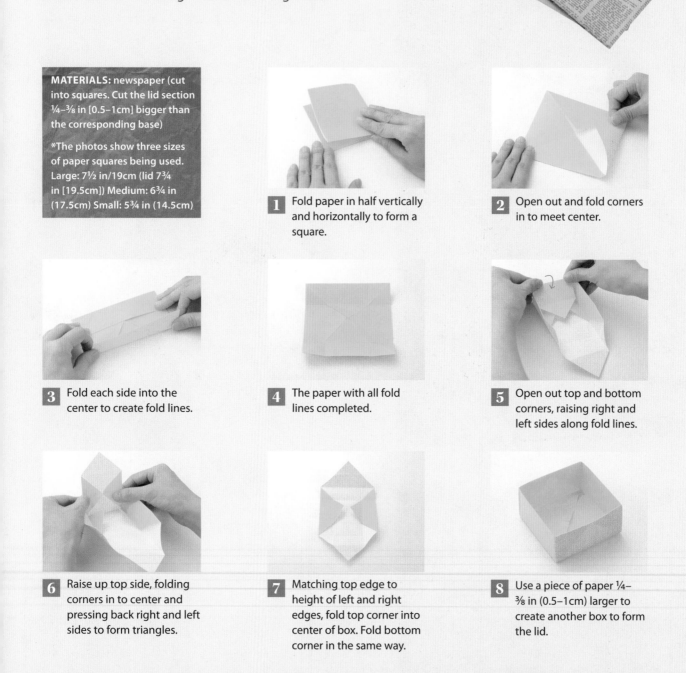

1 Fold paper in half vertically and horizontally to form a square.

2 Open out and fold corners in to meet center.

3 Fold each side into the center to create fold lines.

4 The paper with all fold lines completed.

5 Open out top and bottom corners, raising right and left sides along fold lines.

6 Raise up top side, folding corners in to center and pressing back right and left sides to form triangles.

7 Matching top edge to height of left and right edges, fold top corner into center of box. Fold bottom corner in the same way.

8 Use a piece of paper ¼–⅜ in (0.5–1cm) larger to create another box to form the lid.

*On some pages following this, paper that differs from that of the finished item has been used in order to make steps easier to understand.

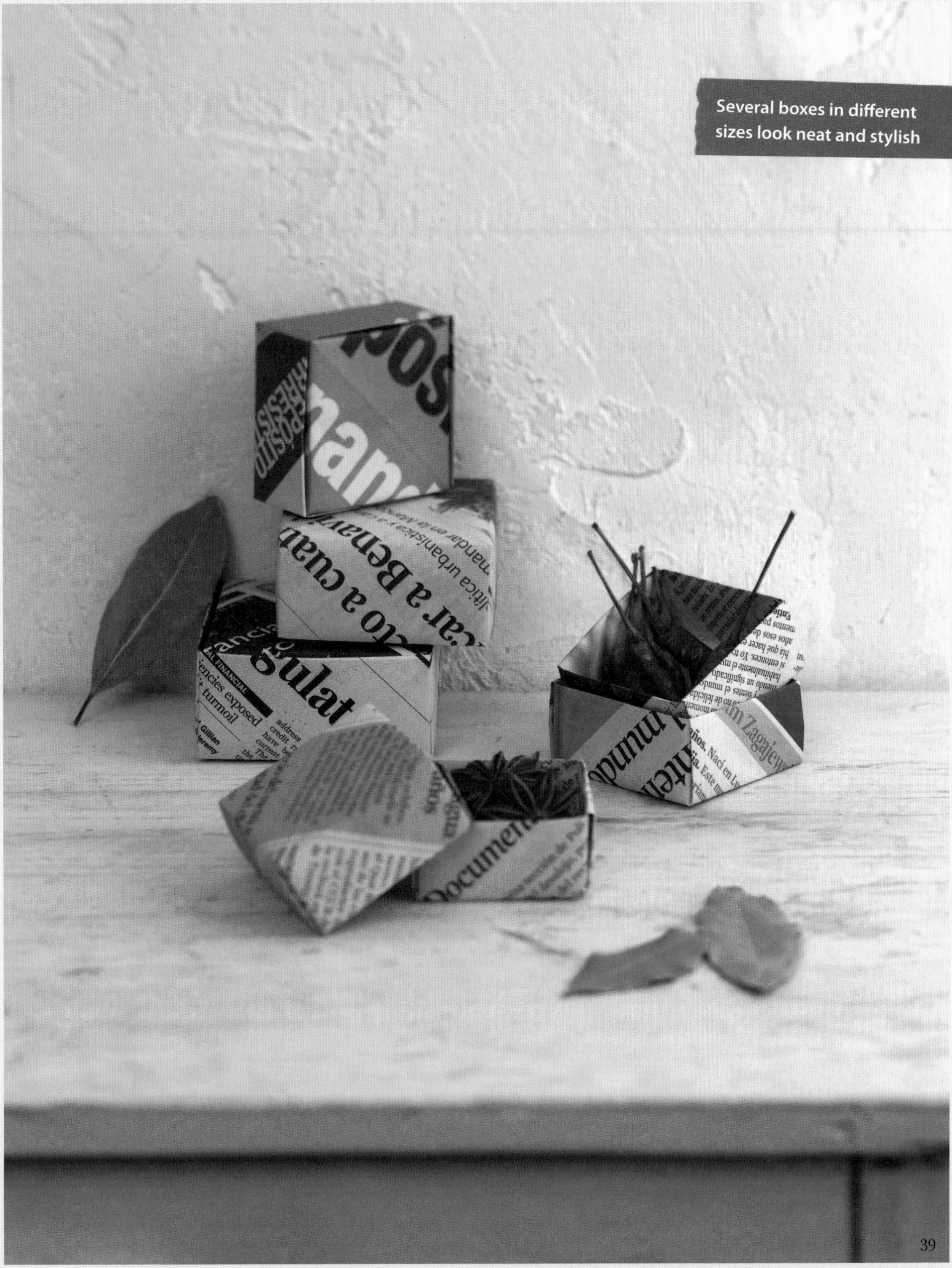

Several boxes in different sizes look neat and stylish

Turn an Envelope into a Tetra Gift Wrapper

At first glance, the recipient of this tetra block will wonder how you folded it. But they're very easy to make—and fun too, so you'll want to make a few. Even business envelopes can be transformed into cute packages like this —perfect for little gifts such as candies and other sundries.

Variations

A mini corsage makes this package special

This tetra block is made from the kind of regular, flat, white bag often seen in shops. A torn-off tag and a corsage (see p31) have been attached with an eyelet.

A tag transforms a manila envelope

Just adding one little detail transforms a manila envelope into gift wrapping. Printed paper has been threaded onto embroidery thread, which is wound around the opening of the envelope and tied at the top.

A tetra block from construction paper

Create a flat bag from origami paper or construction paper (see p62). Making the bag from scratch means you can choose the paper. A label has been attached with a split pin to add an accent.

✱ A split pin has two "prongs" that separate to keep it in place. They can be bought wherever stationery is sold.

MATERIALS: flat paper bag (envelope)

1 In order to create a neat three-sided pyramid-shaped block, first measure out a square.

2 Cut the envelope to the size of a square plus the foldover section.

3 Open mouth of envelope vertically and insert contents.

4 Matching folds on both sides, flatten mouth of envelope to form a tetra block.

5 Fold over mouth of envelope and decorate as you wish.

Packaging Materials Make Great Casual Wrappings

While its usual role is to protect fragile items, with some imagination packaging material works well as casual wrapping with an individual look.

Here, bubble wrap and light corrugated board of the type that is often used between plates form a wrapping arrangement

MATERIALS: bubble wrap (long and wide enough to cover one cup and one saucer), washi tape, curling ribbon

Tip

To make the tape easier to remove, in step 2, fold the end of the tape back on itself to create a small tab.

1 Wrap the saucer in the traditional way for parcels (see p25). Place the cup in the center of the bubble wrap and fold edges into cup.

2 Place cup upside down on top of saucer and wrap cellophane tape once around entire package. Wrap masking tape over top.

3 Wind ribbon around to form a cross (see p84) and curl ends.

Rolled up like a scroll, this package is ready to use as a pencil case!

MATERIALS: corrugated cardboard for winding (width 12 in [30cm], length about 9 in [23cm]), washi tape, wire, button, linen cord

1 Fold up about 2¾ in (7cm) from side. Run a pen along the fold line to make folding easier. Cover edges with washi tape.

2 Pass wire through button and wind through center of right side of cardboard, covering end of wire with tape to secure. Roll up cardboard and wind linen cord around button to fasten.

Unroll the cardboard for a surprise!

43

Baking Paper for a Simple Bouquet

Resistant to oil and water, and with just the right touch of transparency, baking paper is intended for use with food, but can be used to wrap all kinds of items. However, tape does not stick well to it, so it's best used for a method of wrapping that does not require tape.

Variations

A paper napkin adds an accent

A sandwich is given the traditional parcel treatment (see p25). A wooden peg secures a tag and holds the bag closed.

Play up the transparency

A homemade cake is presented in seam line wrapping (see p70). A casual band made from packaging material adds an accent.

MATERIALS: baking paper (cut into a square 1.5 x height of flowers), paper raffia

*Paper other than baking paper can also be used to wrap flowers in this way

Check!
∗ The steps shown here can be applied to other wrapping methods

1 Wrap the stems of the flowers in a damp kitchen towel and aluminum foil and lay on paper to gauge the size you'll need.

2 Cut paper to a square 1.5 x the height of the flowers.

3 Fold paper into a triangle.

Wrapping using a square of paper

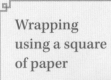

The bouquet on p10 is wrapped in the same way as this one. However, the paper used is left as a square 1.5 x the height of the flowers. If the paper is placed diagonally beneath the flowers when wrapping, the corner of the paper adds an accent, as shown in the photo.

4 Once paper is folded over, fold again in the same direction.

5 Fold over again.

6 Cut a semi circle shape across the bulk of the folds at the base of the triangle.

7 Place flowers on top of the paper, matching the flower heads with the edge of the paper. Fold up bottom edge.

8 Use your right hand to hold paper in place while lifting up the left side of the paper to create a tuck.

9 Cover flowers with left side of paper, then right.

10 Hold bouquet by the stalks and arrange the flowers and paper.

11 Bind the bouquet tightly with paper raffia at the top of the stalks.

12 Tie raffia in a single loop (see p88).

Paper Cups and Egg Cartons Create a Lunch Box

What's inside!? This lunch wrapping really packs a punch. Isn't this a fun idea for when you're taking lunch to someone? The paper cups have been used to hold salad.

MATERIALS: paper cup, elastic cord

1 Press the mouth of the cup flat.

Variations

A cute transformation!

For this project, we made holes at the edge of the carton, threaded wire through and attached the button. Then we tied colored elastic to the button and wound it around the carton to secure a sheet of wax paper.

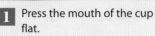

Tip

Swivel the cup around four times as you work to create fold lines, as this makes it easier to create the desired shape.

2 Crush the cup again to bring the fold lines created in step **1.** to the center, then change angles twice more while crushing cup mouth.

3 Pinch both sides of the cup between thumb and forefinger and gradually bring in to center to form a cross shape.

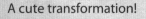

Swap a tag for a fork

The mouth of a paper cup is flattened, and a hole is made in the center to thread cord through. A wooden fork tied to the cup creates an accent.

4 Wind elastic or cord around in a cross shape (see p84) and tie firmly.

Glass Jars Make Reusable Wrappings

Empty jelly, juice and dressing jars lying around the house are perfect for wrapping. Dress up a dressing bottle and add a single stem to create a gift.

B

A

Variations

Make cute decorations for the lid, too

When the jar is unwrapped, a witty message is revealed on the lid! Adding a message covers the original labeling, thereby killing two birds with one stone.

A stamp is a versatile tool for wrapping. How can you use it?

Stationery stores and stores selling ingredients for homemade goods sell all kinds of stamps with fun motifs. And you're not limited to stamping on paper—there's ink for printing on fabric, leather, ceramics, glass and more. Stamps are a handy tool for when your wrapping needs that little something extra, so build up a collection to have on hand. Here, we used glass ink to turn an empty jar into a gift.

A — see "create a circle from the square paper" on p45.

A

MATERIALS: empty jar, cloth (cut in circle double the diameter of the lid), cord

1 Cut as per "create a circle from the square paper" on p45.

2 Keeping the balance between the lid and the fabric size in mind, cut around edges of fabric with pinking shears.

3 Stamp fabric, glass and anything else you want to decorate. Place fabric over lid and wind cord around to secure.

B

MATERIALS: glass bottle (photo shows a dressing bottle), baking paper or glassine paper (cut into a square—sides should be a little longer than the bottle's height)

1 Place bottle in center of paper. Making tucks to match the paper to the bottle shape, raise the paper up around the bottle.

2 Tie two types of cord around neck of bottle.

A Collage from Recycled Wrapping Paper

Some stores' paper packaging are simply too cute to throw away. Transform the pieces you've kept into a collage to use as wrapping paper! For best results, try to use pieces on which the store name is not too obvious.

Variations

Paper bags are collage materials too

The prints and patterns on paper bags are emphasized in this collage, with tissue paper added inside the bag for an accent. The handles of paper bags can be reused too, so don't throw them away!

Triangle wrapping looks charming whatever paper you use

Triangle wrapping is a cute way of wrapping where a fold resembles the roof of a house. The waffles on p5 are wrapped in this way. To give the triangle a neater shape, use paper with some thickness to it, such as scrapbooking paper. This method of wrapping allows the contents to be seen, so for candy and other small items, it's a good idea to wrap them in cellophane or tissue paper first.

This is the same wrapping!

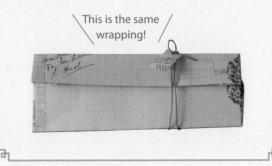

MATERIALS: recycled wrapping paper (stuck together to form square with sides measuring 12 in [30.5cm]), sticker
*If the base is unstable, cut a piece of card 9¾ in x 3¼ in (24.5cm X 8cm) and place inside

1 Place double-sided tape on left edge of paper measuring 6¾ in (17cm) wide x 12 in (30.5cm) long.

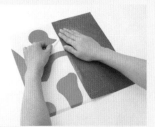

2 Place paper measuring 5¾ in (14.5cm) wide x 12 in (30.5cm) long over first piece of paper, allowing ⅜ in (1cm) overlap.

3 Place paper measuring 1½ in (4cm) wide x 10 in (25cm) high over center to hide join (even though other paper is 12 in (30.5cm) long).

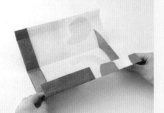

1¼ in (3cm) 1¼ in (3cm) 1¼ in (3cm) 1¼ in (3cm)

4 Fold in 1¼ in (3cm) on all sides.

5 Fold left, right and top sides along 1¼ in (3cm) fold lines in that order, then fold into thirds vertically to create fold lines.

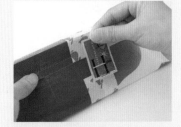

6 Fold along lines to bring top and bottom edges of paper together to create triangular tent shape. Pinch in both sides of triangular "tent" base to make firm.

7 Slide long edge of paper into folded over section and attach sticker.

51

Even More Recycled Wrappings

Regardless of the material, you are only limited by your own ideas when it comes to creating casual, individual wrapping. Look to items close to hand and let your imagination run wild!

Candy packet

A candy packet goes girly

Run cord around the opening of a candy packet and fold it over a few times. Bring the edges up to meet and tie the cord.

A mini-pouch you'll want to give to children

To match the pop mood of the candy packet, a colorful ribbon is threaded through the folded-over packet opening and tied at the edge.

Calendar

What's inside this little box of secrets?

The numbers and letters on a calendar can be used to cool effect. This photo shows the small box from p38 worked into a long rectangle shape.

Numbers lend a sophisticated tone to a decorative band

Modern taste is behind this wrapping for a rolled-up towel: a calendar is wrapped around the towel, then baking paper is layered over the top.

chapter
3

Wrapping with Hand-made Materials

Wrapping that's done with the recipient in mind makes the heart sing, but if you can make the wrapping by hand too, there's no end to the enjoyment it will bring. Here we'll show you how to enjoy handmade wrapping, from simple arrangements to proper paper bags with handles.

Mix Materials to Make Tags and Labels

With a little time and effort you can have tags and labels like these. Adding even one to a parcel makes it significantly more stylish, so they're a great weapon to have in your wrapping arsenal.

Add little touches to simple parcels to create original wrapping

Tags

Leather & fabric

Both fabric and leather are stamped, with the outline on the leather cut-out, creating an antique air.

Printed materials & old photos

A printed card from a shop and origami paper are cut to create tags, and a cut-out image taken from a holiday snap is added.

Slip of paper & button

A ticket stub from overseas is matched with leftover wrapping paper, with a red button added for color.

Old postcard & baking paper

An image from an old postcard is shrunk on a photocopier and matched with stamped baking paper, the great multi-tasking material. The little trick of curling up the paper is effective here.

Banner

Fabric, printed material & an old stamp

A label is attached directly to the wrapping to add an accent. Canvas fabric, printed material from overseas and an old stamp are used to create the label, which can be made to quite a large size if you like.

A Basic Method for Creating Tags

It's not necessary to match materials when making tags—simply cut paper and run cord through a hole, and you're done.

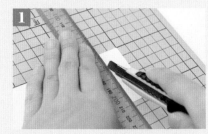

1 Cut light-medium thick card to desired size.

2 Use a hole punch to create a hole in the center of one end of the card. Adding a ring reinforcement sticker will prevent tearing and create an accent.

3 Run ribbon or cord through hole. Write a message on the tag and attach to parcel.

Easy-to-make Wrapping Paper

When you need to wrap a gift but can't find the right kind of wrapping paper, try making your own original paper. With the help of a photocopier, stamps and everyday papers, in no time at all you'll have wrapping paper to treasure.

A

B

C

D

Use photocopies and stamps to create world exclusive wrapping paper

A

Color Photocopies

Turn fabric and printed matter into paper

With the help of a color photocopier, your favorite fabric or printed matter can be turned into wrapping paper in colors true to the original material. As it comes in such a variety of patterns and colors, fabric works particularly well. The paper shown is a color copy of flower-print fabric.

B

Stamps

Create a pattern using lots of stamps

The photo shows a paper napkin which has been stamped. Use plain paper and scatter different stamps all over it or join up the same motif to create something unique.

C

Hand-drawn Designs

World exclusive wrapping paper

Here, a leaf pattern has been drawn using colored pencil. Use crayon, paint or whatever you like to draw a design. Even just adding color to paper, such as for the necktie wrapping on p13, can create an interesting effect. We recommend using paper that has some texture to it.

D

Monochrome Photocopies

Maps, letters and the like look cool even in monochrome

Things like maps of foreign countries or English letters look classy even in black and white. Using colored paper creates a different effect, so give it a try.

Use a Photocopier like a Pro

As seen over the previous pages, photocopies are indispensable for creating original materials.

If you make use of the various functions on a photocopier such as "repeat", "reverse" and "monochrome," you can transform even one material into all kinds of paper and wrapping material. It's a good idea to put aside everyday bits and pieces that can be used for photocopying material.

Tickets and pamphlets from overseas. Old printed matter, stamps and so on are available to buy on the internet, among other sources.

Dyed Paper for an Antique Look

If steeped in black tea or coffee, paper takes on an antique appearance and texture. In particular, doilies treated in this way add the perfect accent to wax paper or craft paper wrapping.

Perfect packaging for handmade gifts

Although it's simple, this wrapping has a sweet, girly air to it. To create it, the mouth of a wax paper bag was folded over, then a doily folded in half was placed over the bag and linen cord tied in a V shap was added (see p86).

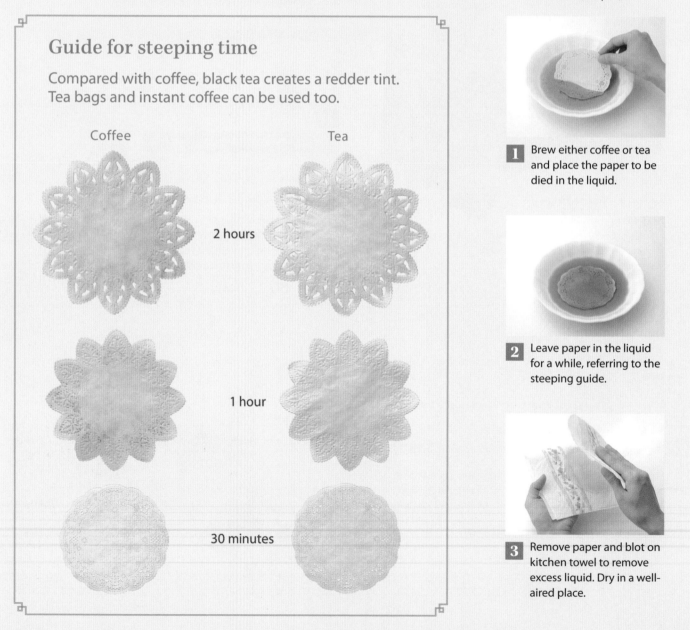

Guide for steeping time

Compared with coffee, black tea creates a redder tint. Tea bags and instant coffee can be used too.

Coffee   Tea

2 hours

1 hour

30 minutes

1 Brew either coffee or tea and place the paper to be died in the liquid.

2 Leave paper in the liquid for a while, referring to the steeping guide.

3 Remove paper and blot on kitchen towel to remove excess liquid. Dry in a well-aired place.

Favorite Papers
Get the Wax Treatment

Here, we've used melted candle wax to create original wax paper. The process is simple, but large pieces of paper require some time and effort, so use it for paper just to add an accent. It lends a unique texture to regular paper.

An accent for wrapping with the gift contents on show

A photocopy of a London metro map has been transformed into wax paper. It's used as a wrapping band with a ribbon tied over the top. This kind of wrapping is superb for a casual gift where you'd like the contents to be seen.

Totally transformed texture!

On the left is the paper prior to the wax treatment, while the right is the "after" photo. The color is more intense and the paper has more texture.

MATERIALS: candle, baking paper (to cover the paper to be treated)

1 Shave candle over baking paper.

2 Rather than shaving off a large quantity at once, add candle wax little by little to cover the paper.

3 Fold baking paper in two and iron over the top to melt wax.

4 When wax has melted, place paper to be treated inside baking paper.

5 Iron over top of baking paper again, making sure to spread out wax evenly over entire sheet of paper.

Make a Cut-and-paste Collage Box

Decorate an empty box with all sorts of items to create a collage box. If done neatly, the box won't even require wrapping! Try using items like recycled wrapping paper, washi tape, photos and photocopies of printed matter—whatever materials you want to use are fine.

Achieving this effect is as simple as sticking on your favorite materials

A present box that needs no wrapping

Just like a little treasure chest, this box needn't be wrapped. Use some balled-up tissue paper as a base layer before adding presents to create the look of a gift from overseas.

Variations

Create a collage on an empty cheese box

Only the lid of this empty cheese box has been decorated with an antique-style collage, the main feature of which is the three-dimensional butterfly.

MATERIALS: empty box, printed matter or photocopied photos, washi tape and other such collage materials

1 Prepare materials that could be used for collage. It's a good idea to gather plenty of items.

2 Cut out photos and printed matter into desired shapes.

3 Cut out printed matter to match the size of the box and attach to the lid using double-sided tape.

4 Cover main part of box with washi tape, combining different sizes and patterns of tape.

5 Place items for collage on lid and consider placement, keeping overall balance in mind.

6 Apply washi tape to box.

7 Add photos and photocopies using glue or double-sided tape.

Lots of Paper Bags to Make

With just paper and double-sided tape, it's surprisingly easy to make a paper bag or packet. This paper bag with a base is made so well it looks just like something from a store! Try using recycled wrapping paper, attractive printed materials or photocopied fabric to create original paper bags.

B

A

They're so simple to make that you'll want to create several to hold all kinds of things

A

MATERIALS: paper (width: twice the size of the finished product + ¾ (2cm) for flap at base; length: finished size + ⅜ in (1cm) for flap) *The item shown is made from a 6¾ in (17.5cm) square of origami paper

1 Fold in ⅜ in (1cm) of right edge of paper to create a narrow margin fold.

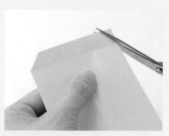

2 Fold in right side of paper along the width, bringing it to the center. Stick double-sided tape to margin fold.

3 Fold in left side along the width of paper to overlap by ⅜ in (1cm) at center. Fold over right side and stick down.

4 Fold up bottom edge by ⅜ in (1cm).

5 Trim off the corners of the flap and the inner edge of the flap (the side that will stick to the body of the packet).

6 Attach double-sided tape to entire flap. Fold over and stick into place.

B

MATERIALS: paper (width: twice the size of the finished product + 2 x gusset width + ⅜ in (1cm) for flap; length: size of finished product)

Making a flat bag

The bag on the left on p62 doesn't have side gussets, but it's just as cute. The steps for making it are the same as for the bag with gussets up to step 5.

1 Fold in ⅜ in (1cm) of left edge. Fold paper in half and use double-sided tape to join edges.

2 Fold up bottom by the width of the base + the flap size (about ¼ of the length of the bag, or in the bag shown here, 2¼ in [6cm]).

3 Open out and press both sides into triangles.

4 Create fold lines by folding paper so edges overlap ⅜ in (1cm) over center line.

Center line

5 Place double-sided tape on base as per photo and fold in first the edge closest to you, folding the other edge over the top.

6 Create fold lines along edges to form rectangular base shape. Open out bag and neaten shape by pressing along fold lines.

Make a Casual Gift Envelope

While it wouldn't be used for formal occasions, this subtly chic gift envelope is great for giving money as a gift.

Whether the amount is large or small, this envelope will show your thoughtfulness

A

MATERIALS: paper 8¾ in (22cm) square, paper to add an accent (width: ¾ in [2cm], length: 8¾ in [22cm]), cord

1 Fold paper vertically into equal thirds.

2 Fold in to ⅜ in (1cm) along right side to create margin fold, then fold again 1¼ in (3cm) in from folded edge.

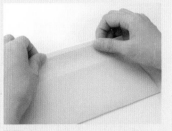

3 Bring fold line created in step **2** to ⅜ in (1cm) from edge and create tuck.

4 Turn over and fold on fold line created in step **1**.

5 Place double-sided tape on margin fold. Slip in strip of accent paper and press down lightly over tape.

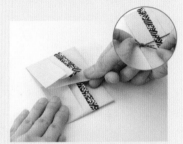

6 Fold over top edge by 2¼ in (6cm). Fold bottom edge over it. Turn over and tie cord on front of envelope.

B

MATERIALS: paper 8¾ in (22cm) square, paper to add an accent (width: 3¼ in [8cm], length: 6¼ in [16cm]), cord

1 Fold paper in half so left and right corners are parallel to one another.

2 Fold both layers of right side over to match to left side.

3 Cut accent paper to match internal triangle shape.

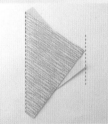

4 Stick accent paper from step **3** to internal triangle shape and cover with outer triangle.

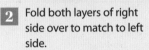

5 Turn over and fold top edge down ⅜ in (1cm).

⅜ in (1cm)

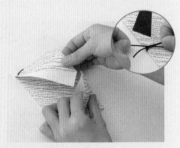

6 Slip top edge into bottom fold and tie cord on front of envelope.

Make a Paper Bag with Handles

Just like a mini handbag, this paper bag with handles is finished off beautifully with tissue paper on the inside. What's more, it's made from two layers of paper, so it's sturdy. The handles are recycled from other paper bags, but you can use the bag without handles too!

So sturdy it can be used like a mini handbag

MATERIALS: paper (width: 15¾ in [40cm], length: 13¼ in [35cm]), cardboard (width: 7 in [18cm], length: 1¼ in [3cm]), tissue paper to wrap around cardboard

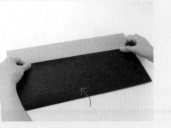

1 Lay paper with outer-facing side facing up and fold up 14cm from bottom edge.

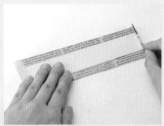

1¼ in (3cm)

Pocket section

2 Bring folded edge up 1¼ in (3cm) and press to form pocket section.

Check!
For a bag without pockets, start here!

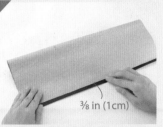

⅜ in (1cm)

3 Turn over and fold so paper on top meets paper on bottom ⅜ in (1cm) in from bottom edge. Create fold line ⅜ in (1cm) in from bottom edge.

4 Fold left and right edges in by ⅜ in (1cm). Fold widthways along center.

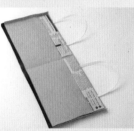

5 Create handles. First, wrap card in tissue paper and glue tissue paper to card.

6 Stick handles to cardboard 1⅜ in (3.5cm) from ends.

7 Stick double-sided tape to top and bottom edge of cardboard (a ⅜ in (1cm) width tape is recommended). Create a set of two handles.

8 Stick handles to paper about 1/16–⅛ in (2–3mm) from top edge, positioning handles at what will be the center of the finished bag.

9 Place double-sided tape along margin fold on right side and stick both sides together.

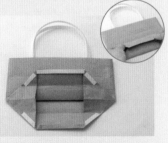

10 Fold 2¼ in (6cm) from bottom. Fold edges to inside along fold lines created in step **3**.

11 Open out left and right edges of base and press into triangle shapes. Fold top and bottom edges of base so they overlap by ⅜ in (1cm) at center.

12 Stick double-sided tape to case at positions shown and press first the bottom edge into position, pressing the top edge over it to complete base.

Wrapping Gifts of Various Sizes Together

When giving several gifts of different sizes together, try this gorgeous wrapping!
The stack of gifts is kept tied together with a wide ribbon.

It's fine to wrap all the presents in the same paper for a uniform effect, but using different colors and patterns, as shown here, creates a more individual look.

1 Wrap each present in desired paper.

2 With larger objects at the bottom, stack presents and tie ribbon around them in a cross shape (see p84).

3 Tie ribbon in a triple loop (see p88) and puff out bow to finish.

chapter
4

Techniques for Beautiful Gift Wrapping

How do you wrap a box neatly? And how do you achieve a beautiful bow? Here you'll find wrapping techniques using boxes, wrapping paper and ribbon that can be used for both casual and formal occasions. These are the essentials of wrapping. A firm grasp of these basic methods will help when trying out different wrapping ideas and arrangements.

Seam Line Wrapping

As it's simple and uses relatively little paper compared with other wrapping methods, this type of wrapping is recommended even for beginners. Enjoy adding tucks to form different arrangements. This style of wrapping is also called caramel wrapping.

B

A

This basic wrapping is the first style you should learn

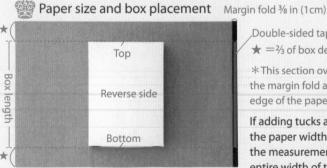

Paper size and box placement

Margin fold ⅜ in (1cm)

Top

Reverse side

Bottom

Box length

★

★

Measurement around entire width of box + ¾–1¼ in (2–3cm)

Double-sided tape
★ = ⅔ of box depth

✻ This section overlaps over the margin fold and the other edge of the paper

If adding tucks as per box B, the paper width needs to be the measurement around the entire width of the box + width of tucks (=width of margin fold) x 3 x number of tucks.

Deep boxes can be wrapped in this way too

The paper size and box placement are the same as the basic type for this kind of box.

A

1 Bring right edge of paper to center of box, then bring left edge of paper over.

2 Layer right edge of paper over left, joining by removing backing from double-sided tape a little at a time and pressing edges together.

3 Fold top and bottom edges of paper to neatly cover box. All edges should be pressed into triangles.

4 Fold bottom edge in toward box. Press so that triangle shapes form on the outer side of the paper.

5 Fold the outer side of the paper back toward you at the center of the box breadth to create a fold line, then turn over to inside in a margin fold.

6 Stick together with double-sided tape. Fold and stick the top edge of the wrapping in the same way.

Finished!

B (Tucks)

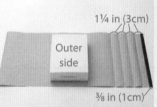

1¼ in (3cm)

Outer side

⅜ in (1cm)

1 Fold in right edge of paper by ⅜ in (1cm). Create four fold lines 1¼ in (3cm) apart by rolling end of paper toward box and pressing.

2 Turn over so outer side of paper faces you. Create tucks by bringing fold lines created in step 1 to each be ⅜ in (1cm) from edge of the next fold.

3 Secure tucks by sticking cellophane tape over folds on reverse side of paper. Attach double-sided tape to margin fold.

4 Place box on reverse side of paper and position tucked paper over top, bringing edge of tucked side toward left of box to meet other edge.

5 Turn box over and complete wrapping by sticking down top and bottom edges of paper as per steps A3–6.

Finished!

Diagonal Wrapping

Due to the fact that it's the wrapping method used in department stores, this type of wrapping is also called "department store wrapping", and is often employed for formal occasions. There's no need for detailed folding, and once you master it you'll be able to wrap a box very quickly by turning it around as you go.

👑 Paper size and placement

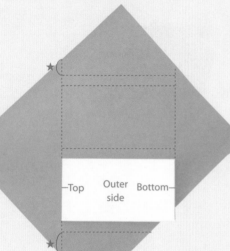

—Top Outer side Bottom—

★ = more than 1/16–1/8 in (2–3cm)
If you're wanting the reverse side of the paper to face out, as per the finished wrapping on the right, place the reverse side facing up when wrapping the box.

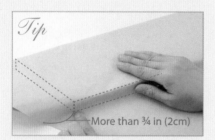

—More than ¾ in (2cm)

The trick to measuring paper size for diagonal wrapping

As shown in step **1**, wrap the edge of paper closest to you over the box, then wrap the edge of paper furthest from you over the box. The lower left corner of the box should be covered at this time. There should be at least ¾ in (2cm) from the corner of the box to the edge of the paper.

1 Bring the paper closest to you over the box to form an isosceles triangle and create room for the lower left corner of the box.

2 Raise up the paper on the left, folding in the excess flat against the box edge in a triangle shape.

3 Bring paper over box, folding in as you go. Make sure the fold of the paper is in line with the edge of the box when you do this.

4 Making sure that the paper is in line with the edge of the box, raise up box, folding paper furthest from you in and placing box over paper.

5 Raise up right edge of paper along edge of box to cover it, folding excess in as you go.

6 Raise up edge of paper farthest from you also, tucking in excess to inner side in a triangle shape.

7 Pull furthest edge of paper to cover box and create fold line, then open out again.

8 Turn box 90 degrees to the right and fold **A** outwards along diagonal line between opposing corners of box, then fold **A** to inside.

9 Fold **B** outwards in line with **A**, then fold to inside.

10 Create fold line along lower edge of **B** to match lower right corner of box, then fold inwards.

Finished!

Pocket

Top

Outer side

Bottom

Secure

Reverse side

A bit of sophisticated packaging —unusual structure and elegant touches

Square Wrapping

This type of wrapping is done without turning the gift box over, so is handy for wrapping items such as cakes or heavy things that can't be flipped. It gets its name from the square paper used for this method.

Diagonal lines form an accent, making this wrapping attractive even without a ribbon!

👑 Paper size and box placement

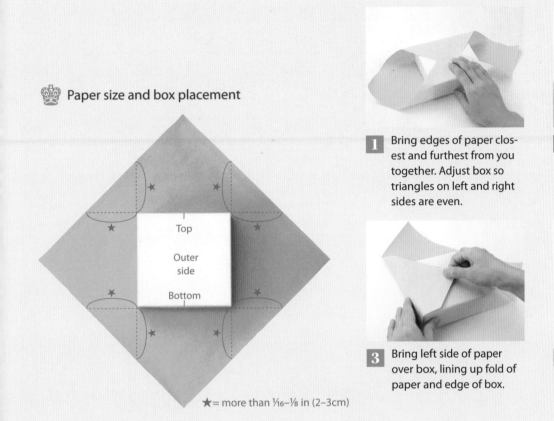

Top

Outer side

Bottom

★ = more than 1/16–1/8 in (2–3cm)

1 Bring edges of paper closest and furthest from you together. Adjust box so triangles on left and right sides are even.

2 Place paper closest to you over box. Raise up left side, tucking in excess paper along edge of box.

3 Bring left side of paper over box, lining up fold of paper and edge of box.

4 Fold just-created section outwards in line with diagonally opposite corner of box to create a fold guide line, then tuck inwards.

5 In the same way, raise up the right side of the paper to cover box, ensuring paper is in line with edge of box. Make a margin fold.

6 With fingers on corners of box furthest from you, raise up paper, folding in excess toward box.

To wrap a rectangular box

Working out the amount of paper needed and the wrapping method are the same for a rectangular box as for a square one. However, the final fold is slightly different.

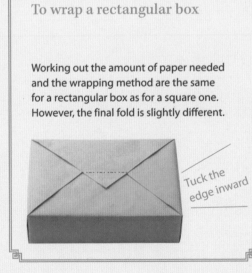

Tuck the edge inward

7 Create margin folds along both edges of the just-folded paper, forming diagonal lines across the box. Use double-sided tape to stick the edge of the paper down.

Finished!

75

Twist and Tie Wrapping

If non-woven fabric, waffle paper or other soft paper is used, this style of wrapping is even easier and creates a soft, gentle effect. It can be used to wrap boxes or containers of all shapes. Tie a ribbon around the parcel for an airy look.

No techniques are required for achieving this splendid finish

👑 Paper size and box placement

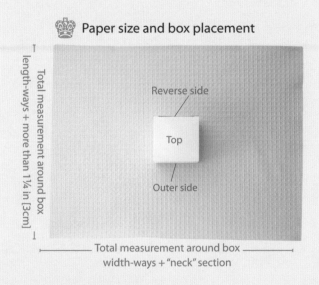

Reverse side

Top

Outer side

Total measurement around box
length-ways + more than 1¼ in [3cm]

Total measurement around box
width-ways + "neck" section

*Photo shows half total measurement around box width-ways

1 Bring together sides of paper closest and furthest from you over top of box.

2 Fold over excess paper and press away from you.

3 Bring up edges of paper, holding down paper at edge of box at the same time. Make sure edges of paper follow the lines of the box.

4 Scrunch paper together over top of box.

Finished!

5 Bring right edge of paper up in the same way and even out gathers at center of box.

6 Neaten "neck" section and attach ribbon.

Pillow Box Wrapping

The seam line wrapping method can be used to wrap pillow boxes also, with a neat finish achieved by following the curves. Small pillow boxes can be used for items such as accessories and candy, while scarves, shirts and other items of clothing can be packaged in larger boxes. This style of wrapping is also called concave wrapping.

The trick is to make the box corners neat

👑 Paper size and box placement

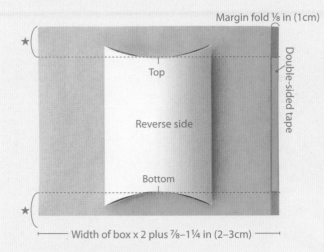

Margin fold ⅛ in (1cm)

★

Top

Reverse side

Bottom

★

Double-sided tape

⊢ Width of box x 2 plus ⅞–1¼ in (2–3cm) ⊣

★= ⅔ box breadth
∗ panel fold + amount of overlap
If adding a pocket, as per the finished package on the right, add 2 x the pocket depth to the size of the basic paper. Follow steps 2–3 for "wrapping that can be used as a book cover" on p92 to make the pocket before starting to wrap the box.

1 Match right side of paper to center of box, then bring left side of paper to cover box also.

2 Place right side of paper over left. Stick together using double-sided tape, removing backing as you go.

3 Fold over bottom edge of paper to match reverse side to box curve, pressing firmly all the way to the corners.

4 Bring up outer side of paper and create fold lines on excess paper on both right and left sides.

5 Tuck paper inwards at fold lines created in step 4.

6 Fold outwards along halfway line of box breadth, then tuck inwards.

7 Attach double-sided tape to panel fold and stick down. Repeat for top edge of box.

Finished!

They're tricky, but when tucks are done well, this kind of wrapping looks beautiful!

Pillar Wrapping

This wrapping is perfect for cylindrical shapes such as tea canisters or tins of candy. Creating tucks around the cylindrical shape can be a bit difficult for beginners, but the beautiful finished result can't be beaten.

Paper size and box placement

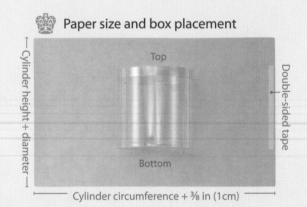

Cylinder height + diameter

Top

Bottom

Double-sided tape

Cylinder circumference + ⅜ in (1cm)

1. If the cylinder has a join somewhere along the vertical, line up the right side of the paper with the join as a starting point.

2. Place left side, then right side of paper over cylinder and stick paper together with double-sided tape.

3. Bring bottom left edge of paper to center of cylinder to form a tuck. The first tuck should match up with the join of the paper.

4. Create tucks at equal intervals.

5. To finish, slip edge of paper in under first tuck.

6. Create tucks on top edge in the same way, starting at the point where the paper edges join.

7. Work tucks at top in the opposite direction from the tucks at the base.

8. Be careful not to make layers too thick in the center or to leave a hole.

9. To finish, slip edge of paper under first tuck.

Finished!

Tip

The number of tucks can be adjusted, but this wrapping looks attractive when opposing tucks form a straight line. Once ¼ of the cylinder has been wrapped, if there are three tucks, work to create 12 in total; if there are four tucks, create a total of 16.

Tying a Bow

Adding a ribbon to a parcel gives it a sweet flamboyance. Let's begin by learning the basic way to tie a bow. For patterned ribbons and types with outer and reverse ("right" and "wrong") sides, use little tricks when tying to create a pretty bow that shows off the "right" side of the ribbon.

Aim for a tautly tied, light and airy bow

A

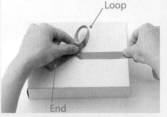  

Loop

End

1 Keeping the overall balance of the box and ribbon in mind, place the ribbon around the box and create one side of the bow to work out how long to cut the ribbon.

2 Holding the box and ribbon from step 1 in your left hand, use your right hand to draw the long end of the ribbon across the box.

3 Place left ribbon over right, running end under right ribbon and pulling up to upper right.

  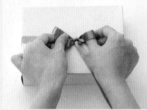 

Finished!

4 Pull both ends of ribbon taut. Bring end of left ribbon toward you to form a loop.

5 Bring ribbon on right over loop from step 4 and fold over. Pass through loop from step 4 and bring up to upper left.

6 Pull up loop to upper left. To tighten, pull on back part of right loop and front part of left loop. Trim ends.

B

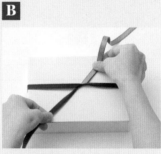  

1 Tie ribbon as per steps A1–3. The right hand holds the ribbon so the reverse side is visible.

2 Pull both sides of ribbon taut. Create loop with left side of ribbon and run right side of ribbon over the top.

3 Wind right side of ribbon over top again.

Finished!

4 Pass loop created in step 3 through first loop and pull up to upper left.

5 Place fingers in loops and pull away from you. Trim ends of ribbon to equal lengths.

Horizontal Single Bow / Vertical Single Bow / Cross Bow

These are the three standard ways to tie ribbons. The single bow gives a more casual impression than the cross bow, but keep the size and function of the box in mind when deciding which bow to use.

A

1 Wind ribbon once around width of box and tie in a bow (see p82).

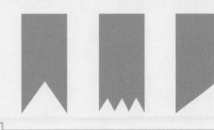

Cut the ribbon ends in different ways for different looks!

There are lots of ways to cut the ends of ribbons, including in a V shape, pinking, or on the diagonal. Choose how to cut the ribbon depending on its width and on the type of wrapping.

B

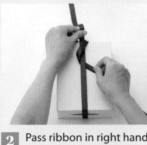

1 Take the length needed for one half of the bow and the ends of the ribbon in the left hand, and with the long end of the ribbon in the right hand, pass it vertically around the box.

2 Pass ribbon in right hand over ribbon in left hand, then pass it under and pull to low.

3 Create loop using ribbon in right hand. Pass ribbon in left hand over loop and then through hole and draw up to upper right.

Finished!

C

1 Follow steps **A1–2** on p83 to wind ribbon once around width of box, then cross left and right sides of ribbon.

Tip

When crossing ribbon over, pull ribbon in right hand down and ribbon in left hand up. Be careful that the ribbon doesn't twist on to the reverse side.

2 Once the ribbon in the right hand has passed vertically around the box from bottom to top, place it over the ribbon in the left hand.

4 Pull ribbon in right hand toward upper right and ribbon in left hand toward lower left.

3 Pass ribbon in right hand under crossover section from lower left to upper right and pull through.

Finished!

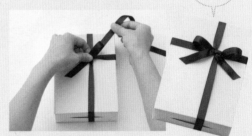

5 Create loop in ribbon in left hand. Place ribbon in right hand over the top and draw loop up to upper left.

Bow Tied on a V / Bow Tied Diagonally

These ways to tie ribbons create a more individual impression
than the standard cross method. The style of bow and its
position can be arranged according to your own taste.
Changing the way the ribbon is tied can really increase
the impact of the wrapping paper.

A

B

Alter the position of the
ribbon for a simple variation

A

1 Take the length needed for one half of the bow and the ends of the ribbon in the left hand, and pass the long end of the ribbon vertically around the box twice.

2 Once the ribbon in the right hand has passed vertically around the box from bottom to top, place it over the ribbon in the left hand.

Finished!

3 Pull ribbon in left hand to upper left, tying ribbon at box edge.

4 Create loop with ribbon in right hand. Place ribbon in left hand over the top, passing under loop through hole and drawing up to upper right.

Variations

Alter the position of the ribbon to create a different impression

Once the bow tied on a V is completed, it's relatively easy to shift the position of the ribbon. Placed at the top of the box, it looks chic, while positioned in the center it creates a fresh, spirited impression.

B

1 Take the length needed for one half of the bow and the ends of the ribbon and wind diagonally around the upper right corner of the box.

2 Using your left hand, hold the short part of the ribbon in position at **A**, passing the rest of the ribbon under the lower right corner of the box with your right hand.

3 Pass ribbon in right hand under box from lower left corner, bringing up and over box to meet ribbon in left hand.

4 Place ribbon in right hand over and then under ribbon in left hand and pull up to upper right.

5 Create loop from ribbon in left hand. Place ribbon in right hand over top to create bow and draw through to upper left.

Finished!

Single Loop / TripleLoop

With the single bow as a foundation, the number of loops in a bow can be altered. Enjoy creating different looks by making bows gorgeous or casual.

B

A

Keep it simple with a single loop or use a triple loop to go gorgeous

A

1 Wind ribbon around box as per steps **A1–4** on p83. Create loop with ribbon in left hand.

2 Place ribbon in right hand over loop, fold over and pass through reverse side of loop, drawing through to upper left.

3 Trim ends. The loop and ends can be arranged to face the other way around if preferred.

B

1 Take the length needed for two loops and the ends of the ribbon in the left hand. Wind ribbon in right hand around box and tie.

2 Using the ribbon in the left hand, create a right loop and a left loop. Place ribbon in right hand over center of loops.

3 Pass the looped ribbon in the right hand under loop, drawing out to upper left and neatening for an overall balance.

Notes on Wrapping Gifts for Celebrations and Condolence Gifts

In some cultures, such as the Japanese culture, certain etiquette is observed when it comes to wrapping gifts for formal occasions. The wrapping methods covered so far are appropriate for wrapping gifts for happy occasions, but for gifts to someone suffering the loss of a loved one, left and right and top and bottom may be reversed. The photos below show the differences between the two types of wrapping for formal occasions.

Seam line wrapping

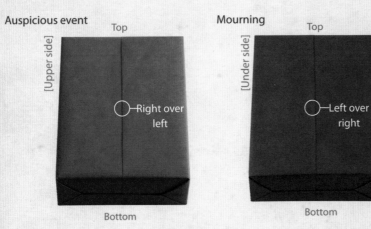

Auspicious event
[Upper side] Top — Right over left — Bottom

Mourning
[Under side] Top — Left over right — Bottom

When using seam line wrapping for a condolence gift the margin fold is on the left and the left side of the wrapping paper should be on top. For diagonal wrapping, wrap a condolence gift in the same way as a gift for an auspicious event, but when placing the box on the paper, place it so the top and bottom face the opposite way. Make sure also to use gray, dark green or other subdued shades of paper for wrapping condolence gifts.

Diagonal wrapping

Reverse side

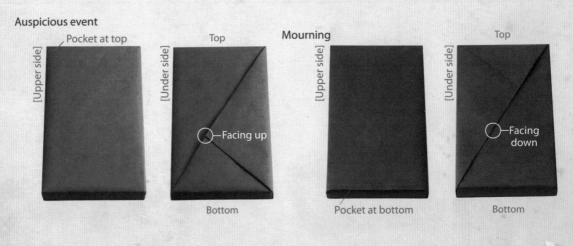

Auspicious event
Pocket at top
[Upper side]
[Under side] Top — Facing up — Bottom

Mourning
[Upper side] Pocket at bottom
[Under side] Top — Facing down — Bottom

Special wrapping lesson
Next-level Techniques

Once you've realized how much fun wrapping can be, think up ideas and arrangements to express your own personality. This lesson should inspire those ideas! Here, the slightly difficult steps for the wrapping on p4–15 are shown.

P4

Wrapping a baked item

MATERIALS: cellophane (width: diameter of cake x 2.5; length: diameter of cake x 3 + height x 2 + 1½ in [4cm]), doily, cord

Direction of cake ↑

¾ in (2cm) wide

1 Fold paper closest to you twice and raise up. Place cake on paper next to folded edge. Slip doily in at back.

2 Bring paper furthest from you over cake and match with edge of paper closest to you.

3 Tape join of paper in several places. Pinch together top left edge of paper.

4 Pinching the peak of the wrapping, press in the paper closest to you toward the cake.

5 Repeat for paper furthest from you and secure in place using tape.

6 Fold in the triangle from the base.

7 Fold the base several times and stick to side of box.

8 Repeat on right side. Turn cake around to opposite side (front) and attach leaf and cord decoration to top right.

∗The glassine paper box that the tart is in is a version of the small box on p38

P7

Accessory wrapping

MATERIALS: transparent bag, heart-shaped doily, wax paper, cord

Cut wax paper to size of bag. Cut out part of center of doily and form cylinder shape, place accessory on cylinder section. Fold doily over wax paper to match size. Place in bag and tie cord in a bow at the top.

P12

Special pom pom ribbon

MATERIALS: organza ribbon x 2 types (each about 59 in [150cm] long), 20 in [50cm] of curling ribbon

1 Place two ribbons together over your hand.

2 Wind ribbons around hand.

3 When ribbons have been wound around 5–6 times, cut at 1¼ in (3cm) from base.

4 Move ribbon around so it is folded ⅝ in (1.5cm) from where it was cut in step **3** (match length with edge of ribbon at start of winding).

5 Snip out triangles on each side of folds at both ends of ribbon loop.

6 Match trimmed sections.

7 Use curling ribbon to tie trimmed sections firmly together.

8 Draw out ribbon from bundle of loops, working alternately from right to left to distribute loops evenly.

9 Twist ribbon at the base when drawing out for fuller, airy loops.

10 Tie ribbon in a cross over box that has been wrapped in the seam line wrapping style (see p70).

11 Place curling ribbon across center of cross. Tie ribbon for box in a bow.

12 Pull curling ribbon so pom pom sits at center of box.

13 Bring other end of curling ribbon under bow toward the front of the box.

14 Tie curling ribbon at front of box to secure pom pom. Tie curling ribbon in a bow.

15 Run ends of curling ribbon along scissor blades to achieve curls.

Special lesson

91

P12
Wrapping that can be used as a book cover

MATERIALS: paper (width: book width x 2 + thickness + 4 in [10cm]; length: book height + pocket depth x 2 + ¾ in [2cm]), ribbon

P14
Wrapping to reveal gifts in a basket

MATERIALS: basket, cellophane (width: width of item to be wrapped + height x 2 + about 8 in (20cm); length: total vertical measurement around item to be wrapped + 8 in [20cm]), tissue paper, ribbon

1 Cut paper and make ⅜ in (1cm) margin folds at top and bottom.

2 Turn paper over so outer side faces up. Match top edge of book with top edge of paper. Decide on position for pocket and fold up where base of pocket will sit.

1 Lay lightly scrunched tissue paper in basket to form base.

2 Place gifts in basket. Place basket on center of cellophane.

3 Fold paper back on itself so bottom edge of book and bottom edge of paper match.

4 Turn paper over to reverse side and place book on top. Fold left side of paper 2 in (5cm) over inside cover of book.

3 Match edges of cellophane furthest from and closest to you above basket.

4 Raise up lower part of left side of cellophane and bring cellophane to center.

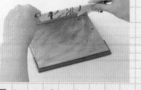

5 Repeat for other side.

6 Tie ribbon around in a vertical single bow (see p84).

5 Gather cellophane together, distributing evenly to form neat shape.

6 Tie ribbon around cellophane in a bow. Repeat for right side.

1 Decorate craft paper however you like and stick to box.

2 Create a panel fold on right side of white paper. Place box on paper and bring right side of paper to center.

3 Create a diagonal fold line starting ⅜ in (1cm) from top of box (this will form the tree shape).

P15

Christmas Wrapping

MATERIALS: white paper (width: total measurement around box + ¾ in (2cm); length: height of box + ⅔ of breadth x 2), craft paper (width: box width; length: box height + breadth), yarn

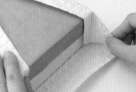

4 Do the same for the left side of the paper.

5 Open out paper and fold inwards along lines created in steps **3** and **4**.

6 With right side on top, match apex points and stick in place using double-sided tape.

7 Using technique for seam line wrapping (see p70), fold in right and left sides at bottom of paper to form triangles.

8 Create panel fold at bottom of paper and stick in place with double-sided tape.

9 Secure top of paper in the same way.

10 Make ⅜ in (1cm) cuts in several places along both sides of tree silhouette.

11 Fold back cuts made in step **10** to form triangles and create tree shape.

12 Wind yarn around two fingers several times.

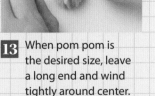

13 When pom pom is the desired size, leave a long end and wind tightly around center.

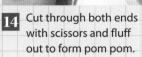

14 Cut through both ends with scissors and fluff out to form pom pom.

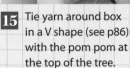

15 Tie yarn around box in a V shape (see p86) with the pom pom at the top of the tree.

16 Tie yarn in a bow under pom pom.

93

Photocopy and use over and over!

Wrapping Extras

Here we've put together stamps, tags and labels that give the perfect finish to wrapping. They can be photocopied and used again and again. Use them to give your wrapping a stylish accent.

*For the tags, we recommend photocopying onto thick paper

Stamps

Tags

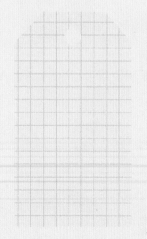

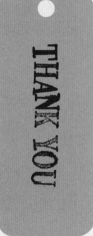

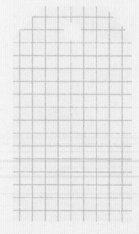

Labels

To

From

enveloppement

Thank you

HAPPY BIRTHDAY

Published in 2015 by Tuttle Publishing, an imprint of Periplus Editions (HK) Ltd.

www.tuttlepublishing.com

ISBN 978-4-8053-1357-2

Japanese Original Title: おしゃれなラッピングレッスン
Oshare na Wrapping Lesson
© Gakken Publishing Co., Ltd. 2010
First published in Japan in 2010 by Gakken Publishing Co., Ltd., Tokyo
English Translation © 2015 Periplus Editions (HK) Ltd.
English translation rights arranged with
GAKKEN PUBLISHING CO., LTD
Through Japan UNI Agency, Inc., Tokyo

Editorial supervisor: Hiroe Miyaoka
Photographer: Kyoko Kozuka
Stylist: Miki Ito (for Tricko)
Illustrator: Kajita Senju (for + Tsukulcoto)
Design and editing by the Three Season Company (Mariko Tsuchiya)

Distributed by

North America, Latin America & Europe
Tuttle Publishing, 364 Innovation Drive,
North Clarendon
VT 05759-9436 U.S.A.
Tel: 1 (802) 773-8930
Fax: 1 (802) 773-6993
info@tuttlepublishing.com
www.tuttlepublishing.com

Japan
Tuttle Publishing, Yaekari Building
3rd Floor, 5-4-12 Osaki
Shinagawa-ku
Tokyo 141 0032
Tel: (81) 3 5437-0171
Fax: (81) 3 5437-0755
sales@tuttle.co.jp
www.tuttle.co.jp

Asia Pacific
Berkeley Books Pte. Ltd.
61 Tai Seng Avenue #02-12
Singapore 534167
Tel: (65) 6280-1330
Fax: (65) 6280-6290
inquiries@periplus.com.sg
www.periplus.com

Printed in Malaysia   1504TW
18 17 16 15   6 5 4 3 2 1

The Tuttle Story
"Books to Span the East and West"

Many people are surprised to learn that the world's largest publisher of books on Asia had its humble beginnings in the tiny American state of Vermont. The company's founder, Charles E. Tuttle, belonged to a New England family steeped in publishing.

Tuttle's father was a noted antiquarian dealer in Rutland, Vermont. Young Charles honed his knowledge of the trade working in the family bookstore, and later in the rare books section of Columbia University Library. His passion for beautiful books—old and new—never wavered throughout his long career as a bookseller and publisher.

After graduating from Harvard, Tuttle enlisted in the military and in 1945 was sent to Tokyo to work on General Douglas MacArthur's staff. He was tasked with helping to revive the Japanese publishing industry, which had been utterly devastated by the war. When his tour of duty was completed, he left the military, married a talented and beautiful singer, Reiko Chiba, and in 1948 began several successful business ventures.

To his astonishment, Tuttle discovered that postwar Tokyo was actually a book-lover's paradise. He befriended dealers in the Kanda district and began supplying rare Japanese editions to American libraries. He also imported American books to sell to the thousands of GIs stationed in Japan. By 1949, Tuttle's business was thriving, and he opened Tokyo's very first English-language bookstore in the Takashimaya Department Store in Ginza, to great success. Two years later, he began publishing books to fulfill the growing interest of foreigners in all things Asian.

Though a westerner, Tuttle was hugely instrumental in bringing a knowledge of Japan and Asia to a world hungry for information about the East. By the time of his death in 1993, he had published over 6,000 books on Asian culture, history and art—a legacy honored by Emperor Hirohito in 1983 with the "Order of the Sacred Treasure," the highest honor Japan can bestow upon a non-Japanese.

The Tuttle company today maintains an active backlist of some 1,500 titles, many of which have been continuously in print since the 1950s and 1960s—a great testament to Charles Tuttle's skill as a publisher. More than 60 years after its founding, Tuttle Publishing is more active today than at any time in its history, still inspired by Charles Tuttle's core mission—to publish fine books to span the East and West and provide a greater understanding of each.